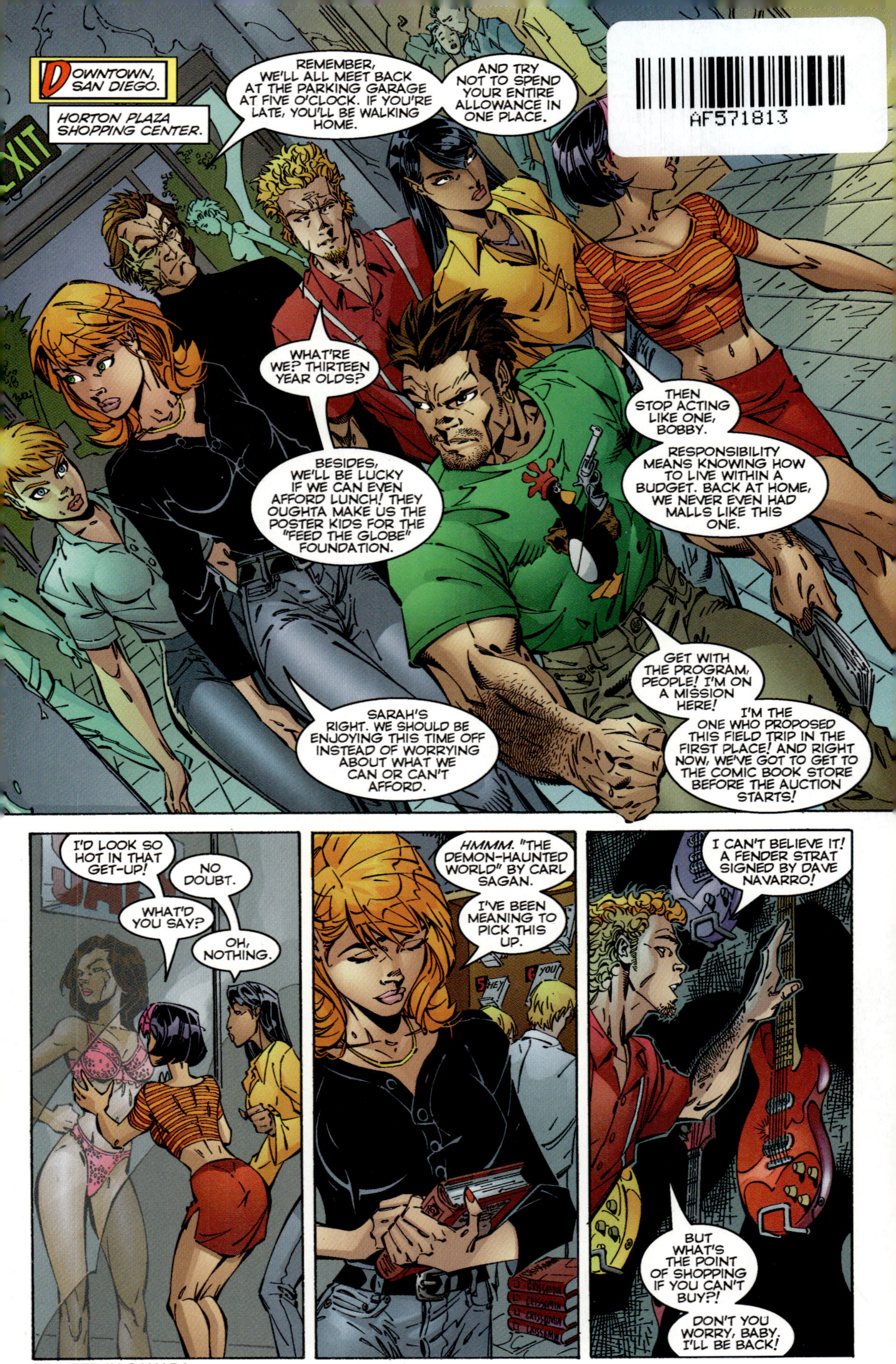

AF571813

DOWNTOWN, SAN DIEGO.

HORTON PLAZA SHOPPING CENTER.

EXIT

REMEMBER, WE'LL ALL MEET BACK AT THE PARKING GARAGE AT FIVE O'CLOCK. IF YOU'RE LATE, YOU'LL BE WALKING HOME.

AND TRY NOT TO SPEND YOUR ENTIRE ALLOWANCE IN ONE PLACE.

WHAT'RE WE? THIRTEEN YEAR OLDS?

THEN STOP ACTING LIKE ONE, BOBBY.

BESIDES, WE'LL BE LUCKY IF WE CAN EVEN AFFORD LUNCH! THEY OUGHTA MAKE US THE POSTER KIDS FOR THE "FEED THE GLOBE" FOUNDATION.

RESPONSIBILITY MEANS KNOWING HOW TO LIVE WITHIN A BUDGET. BACK AT HOME, WE NEVER EVEN HAD MALLS LIKE THIS ONE.

GET WITH THE PROGRAM, PEOPLE! I'M ON A MISSION HERE!

I'M THE ONE WHO PROPOSED THIS FIELD TRIP IN THE FIRST PLACE! AND RIGHT NOW, WE'VE GOT TO GET TO THE COMIC BOOK STORE BEFORE THE AUCTION STARTS!

SARAH'S RIGHT. WE SHOULD BE ENJOYING THIS TIME OFF INSTEAD OF WORRYING ABOUT WHAT WE CAN OR CAN'T AFFORD.

PRINTED IN CANADA

LOOK, PEOPLE! I'M NEVER GONNA MAKE IT TO THE STORE IN TIME IF YOU GUYS KEEP WINDOW SHOPPING --
THAT' S IT! I'M OUTTA HERE!
COMICS
I'VE GOT TO GET THERE BEFORE IT'S...
...TOO LATE!
THE SHOP'S ALREADY PACKED!
THERE IT IS!
Ooooh!
Aaaah!
Whoaa!
STEP RIGHT UP, FOLKS! TAKE A GOOD LOOK AT IT!
IT'S THE BOOK YOU'VE ALL BEEN WAITING FOR!
THAT'S RIGHT, IT'S THE LIMITED EDITION CAPTAIN PYRO CHROMIUM COVER!
IT... IT'S SOOO MINT!
IT MUST BE MINE!
THE ONE AND ONLY COPY AVAILABLE IN THE ENTIRE CITY!
AND THE ONLY WAY TO GET IT IS BY HAVING THE WINNING TICKET!

I DON'T UNDERSTAND WHAT ALL THE FUSS IS ABOUT.
IT MUST BE A GUY THING, KAT.
IT IS JUST A COMIC BOOK, RIGHT?

ACCORDING TO MY DATA BANKS, CAITLIN, THIS PARTICULAR COMIC BOOK IS QUITE RARE.
DUE TO A LIMITED PRINT RUN AND HIGH CONSUMER DEMAND, THIS COMIC BOOK IS PERCEIVED TO BE OF EXCEPTIONAL VALUE.
IN FACT, THE CURENT ASKING PRICE IS APPROXIMATELY $79.95, AT A RATE OF APPRECIATION OF TEN PERCENT A MONTH.

ALL THAT MONEY JUST FOR SOME FUNNY CARTOONS?
YOU KNOW, GRUNGE, I'VE GOT THIS OLD HE-DUDE: MASTER OF THE COSMOS DOLL YOU MIGHT BE INTERESTED IN.

KNOCK IT OFF, GUYS!
THIS IS IMPORTANT TO HIM!
HUH?

BESIDES, COMIC BOOKS AREN'T JUST FOR KIDS ANYMORE. THEY'RE BIG BUSINESS, RIGHT?
SPARE ME THE SARCASM, ROX.
I MEAN, THEY'RE NOT ANY WORSE THAN THOSE SLIPPERY PATH POETRY BOOKS YOU READ.

THAT'S SYLVIA PLATH!
BUT THAT'S NOT WHAT I...
LOOK, I GOTTA BUY MY TICKETS!

...MEANT.
WHY DO YOU *DEAL* WITH HIM, ROXY? HE'S *NEVER* GOING TO GROW UP.

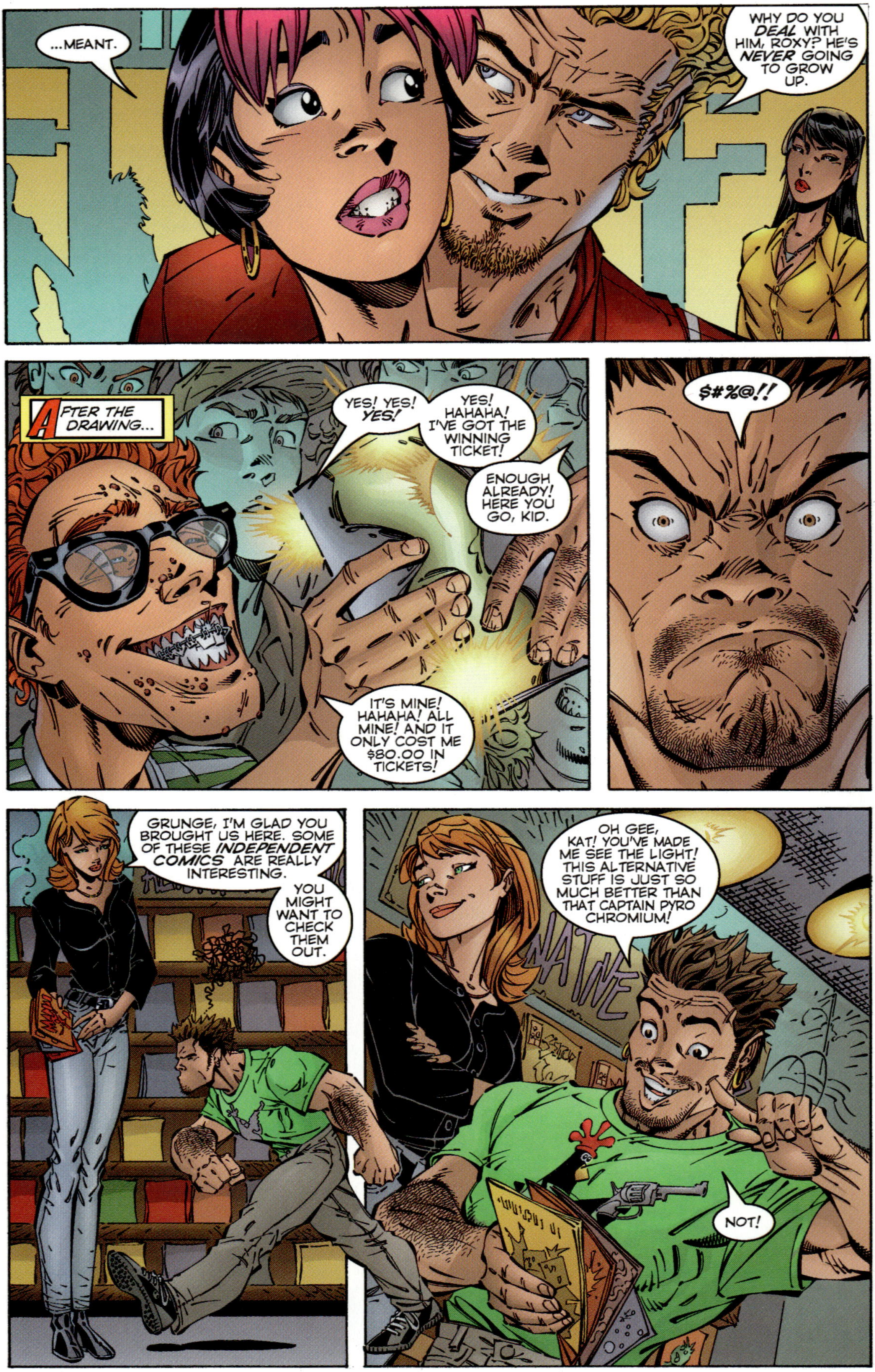

AFTER THE DRAWING...
YES! YES! *YES!*
YES! HAHAHA! I'VE GOT THE WINNING TICKET!
ENOUGH ALREADY! HERE YOU GO, KID.
IT'S MINE! HAHAHA! ALL MINE! AND IT ONLY COST ME $80.00 IN TICKETS!

$#%@!!

GRUNGE, I'M GLAD YOU BROUGHT US HERE. SOME OF THESE *INDEPENDENT COMICS* ARE REALLY INTERESTING.
YOU MIGHT WANT TO CHECK THEM OUT.
OH GEE, KAT! YOU'VE MADE ME SEE THE LIGHT! THIS ALTERNATIVE STUFF IS JUST SO MUCH BETTER THAN THAT CAPTAIN PYRO CHROMIUM!
NOT!

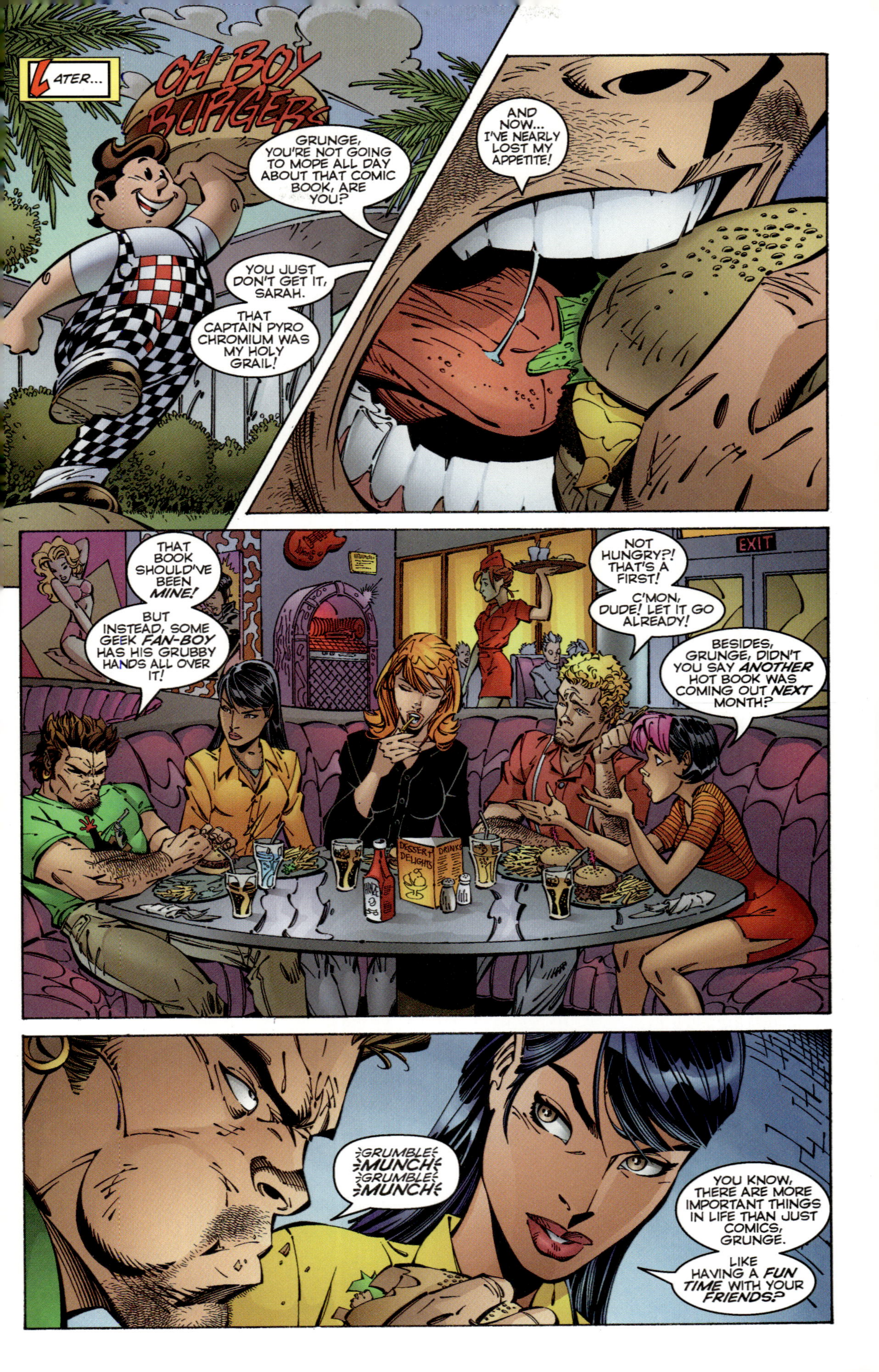

LATER...

OH BOY BURGERS

GRUNGE, YOU'RE NOT GOING TO MOPE ALL DAY ABOUT THAT COMIC BOOK, ARE YOU?

YOU JUST DON'T GET IT, SARAH.

THAT CAPTAIN PYRO CHROMIUM WAS MY HOLY GRAIL!

AND NOW... I'VE NEARLY LOST MY APPETITE!

THAT BOOK SHOULD'VE BEEN *MINE!*

BUT INSTEAD, SOME GEEK *FAN-BOY* HAS HIS GRUBBY HANDS ALL OVER IT!

NOT HUNGRY?! THAT'S A FIRST!

C'MON, DUDE! LET IT GO ALREADY!

BESIDES, GRUNGE, DIDN'T YOU SAY *ANOTHER* HOT BOOK WAS COMING OUT *NEXT* MONTH?

EXIT

DESSERT DELIGHTS

DRINKS

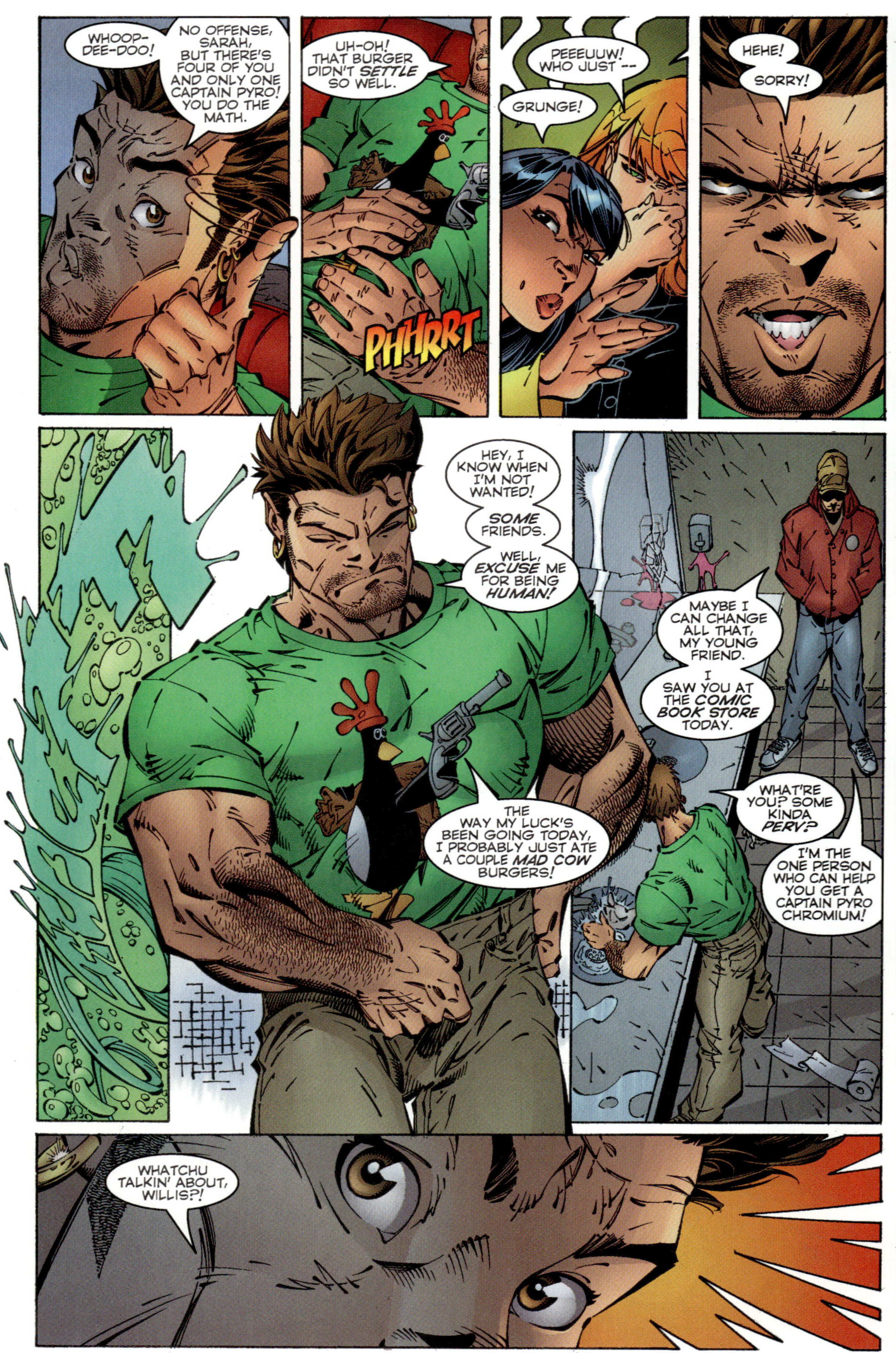
WHOOP-DEE-DOO!
NO OFFENSE, SARAH, BUT THERE'S FOUR OF YOU AND ONLY ONE CAPTAIN PYRO! YOU DO THE MATH.
UH-OH! THAT BURGER DIDN'T SETTLE SO WELL.
PHHRRT
PEEEUUW! WHO JUST --
GRUNGE!
HEHE!
SORRY!
HEY, I KNOW WHEN I'M NOT WANTED!
SOME FRIENDS.
WELL, EXCUSE ME FOR BEING HUMAN!
THE WAY MY LUCK'S BEEN GOING TODAY, I PROBABLY JUST ATE A COUPLE MAD COW BURGERS!
MAYBE I CAN CHANGE ALL THAT, MY YOUNG FRIEND.
I SAW YOU AT THE COMIC BOOK STORE TODAY.
WHAT'RE YOU? SOME KINDA PERV?
I'M THE ONE PERSON WHO CAN HELP YOU GET A CAPTAIN PYRO CHROMIUM!
WHATCHU TALKIN' ABOUT, WILLIS?!

HEHEHE!
THOUGHT THAT MIGHT GET YOUR ATTENTION!
DUDE, ARE YOU --

SERIOUS? WELL, TAKE A GOOD LOOK AT WHAT I'VE GOT RIGHT HERE!
SSHHIINNNG!
THIS IS A ONCE-IN-A-LIFETIME OPPORTUNITY, KID.

THE CHANCE TO MAKE YOUR WILDEST DREAMS COME TRUE!
IF I'M DREAMIN', DON'T WAKE ME UP, PAL!

AND ALL I ASK FOR IN RETURN...
ASK AWAY, DUDE!
...IS YOUR ETERNAL SOUL!
UHHH... SURE!
YOU GOT IT!

IS THAT IT? PANT PANT DO I GET IT NOW?!

TWO THOUSAND YEARS LATER, GRUNGE. WHAT WERE YOU DOING IN THERE?
AND WHY ARE YOU SMILING LIKE THAT? OR SHOULD I EVEN BOTHER ASKING?
CHECK IT OUT, ROX!
IS THAT A CAPTAIN PYRO CHROMIUM?!
BUT HOW'D YOU GET IT?! THE STORE ONLY HAD ONE COPY.
GRUNGE, YOU DIDN'T TAKE IT FROM THE GEEK, DID YOU?
NAH, SOME DUDE IN THE BATHROOM GAVE IT TO ME.
HE'S RIGHT BEHIND -- HEY, WHERE'D HE GO?
UH, A GUY IN THE COMMODE IS GIVING AWAY COMIC BOOKS?
MAN, DIDN'T KNOW YOU WERE INTO THAT STUFF, GRUNGE.
WELL, HE WAS KINDA WEIRD IN A FAUSTIAN SORT OF WAY, BUT...
...UH-OH... DON'T...FEEL... SO...GOOD...
...MUST'VE BEEN... SOMETHING...
...I ATE...
GRUNGE?!
HE -- HE'S PASSED OUT!
WHUMP
WHAT'S WRONG WITH HIM?
...THINK IT WAS THE BURGERS...
...POSSIBLY FOOD POISONING...
...SOMEBODY CALL 911...
GRUNGE?

UNNHH...
...CAPTAIN PYRO...MUST HAVE...CHROMIUM COVER...
...DREAM... COME TRUE...
HEY! YOO-HOO!
GRUNGE! WAKE UP!
EVERYTHING -- STILL -- SPINNING!
WHA--WHAT'S GOING ON?!
WHERE AM I?
YOU'RE IN THE LAND OF S.A.
S.A.?
SEQUENTIAL ART.
OH... RIGHT.
HUH?! WHO -- WHAT'RE YOU?!
MY NAME IS TINKER FALL AND I'VE BEEN SENT TO HELP YOU.
YOU KNOW, YOU REMIND ME OF SOMEBODY.
SO, WHO SENT YOU TO HELP ME?
THE GOOD WITCH. SHE SAID YOU'D NEED HELP FINDING THE GREAT WIZARD.
THE GOOD WITCH?! THE GREAT WIZARD?!
THAT'S IT! THIS IS JUST TOO WHACKED! I GOTTA GET OUT OF HERE!
SOMEBODY WAKE ME UP!
IF YOU REALLY WANT TO GET BACK HOME, GRUNGE, THE GREAT WIZARD OF S.A. IS THE ONLY ONE WHO CAN HELP YOU!

OUR JOURNEY BEGINS HERE.
RIVERDALE HIGH SC
RIVERDALE HIGH?
YOU SURE ABOUT THIS, TINKER FALL?
WHERE ELSE WOULD YOU GO TO LOOK FOR ANSWERS?
WELL, I NEVER SEEMED TO FIND ANY AT SCHOOL.
REALLY? WHAT A SURPRISE.
OH MY!
WHOA! CHECK IT OUT!
IT -- IT'S REALLY!
IT'S ARCHIE AND HIS GANG!
I USED TO READ ALL ABOUT 'EM WHEN I WAS A KID!
RONNIE!
I'VE NEVER SEEN HIM AROUND BEFORE!
HI THERE! WELCOME TO RIVERDALE HIGH!
MY NAME'S ARCHIE AND THESE ARE MY FRIENDS.
YOU ASK ME, HE LOOKS LIKE TROUBLE.
WHAT KIND OF GUY WEARS A PENGUIN ON HIS SHIRT?
I KINDA DIG IT, REGGIE!
BESIDES, HE LOOKS MORE LIKE A BURGER MAN TO ME!
THAT'S ALL YOU EVER THINK ABOUT, JUGHEAD!
JUST LOOK AT HIM, BETTY! THOSE CLOTHES!
HE COULDN'T BE FROM AROUND HERE.
C'MON, EVERYBODY!
IT'S TIME TO CRUISE ON OVER TO POP'S AND GET SOMETHING TO EAT!

YOU KNOW, ARCH. I HAD YOU GUYS PEGGED ALL WRONG.
YOU GUYS ARE MONEY!
MONEY?
COOL.
POPS
OH. THANKS.
WE THINK YOU'RE MONEY, TOO.

POPS
SO YOU'RE ON SOME KIND OF QUEST, HUH?
WELL, THAT'S WHAT TINKER FALL TOLD ME.
MY GUARDIAN FAIRY.
TINKER FALL?
OH...OF COURSE.
POP'S MENU
WOW!
THIS GUY EATS AS MUCH AS JUGHEAD.

MUNCH
NOT MUNCH FOR MUCH MUNCH LONGER.
I'M MUNCH STUFFED!
JUG HERE MUNCH IS THE MAN!

BUT I AM GONNA HURL IF WE DON'T GET SOME NEW TUNES!
DON'T YOU HAVE ANY CUTTING EDGE STUFF?
LIKE WHAT?
HOW ABOUT SOME B***H*** SURFERS?

GIGGLE! GIGGLE!
DON'T MIND, ARCHIE!
RONNIE AND I'LL BE GLAD TO FIND SOME SONGS FOR YOU!
GIGGLE! GIGGLE!

THOSE CHICKS ARE FINE!
SO, WHAT'S THE STORY?
STORY?!
UMMM, WE'RE JUST FRIENDS.
FRIENDS?!
ARE YOU BLIND?
THEY'RE TOTAL BABES!
I THINK I MIGHT JUST HANG HERE FOR A WHILE AND GET TO KNOW 'EM BETTER --
THWACK
WE DON'T HAVE TIME FOR THIS!
YOU'RE SUPPOSED TO BE LOOKING FOR THE WIZARD!
OWWW!
ARE YOU ALL RIGHT, GRUNGE?
I--I THINK TINKER FALL GOT A LITTLE JEALOUS.
THE FAIRY, RIGHT?
JUST HUMOR HIM, JUGHEAD!
WHATEVER YOU SAY, GRUNGE!
YOU'RE G.O. WITH US... ER...OR IS THAT O.G?
UH, THANKS ARCHIE. I THINK.
HEY, BETTY!
I GOTTA BE JETTIN' SOON SO HOW ABOUT YOU AND ME...PSST! PSST! PSST!
I'D NEVER DATE YOU!
SLAP!
AND NEITHER WOULD I!
SLAP!

HA HA HA HA
C'MERE, PAL! I'LL HELP YOU OUT.
YOU'RE LOOKING FOR THE GREAT WIZARD, RIGHT? I HEARD THAT HE'S HANGING OUT WITH ALL THE REALLY HOT CHICKS OVER IN THE *VALLEY OF THE DOLLS!*

VALLEY OF THE *DOLLS?!*
HEY, NOW THAT SOUNDS LIKE *MY* KINDA NEIGHBORHOOD!

C'MON, GRUNGE! TIME TO GO FIND THE WIZARD!
TINKER FALL SAYS WE'VE GOTTA BOAT!
SEE YA AND THANKS FOR ALL THE HELP!
HEHE! THE *FAIRY* AGAIN, HUH?
WELL, YOU BE SURE AND LISTEN TO HER.
REGGIE! YOU *SHOULDN'T* HAVE DONE THAT.

WHAT DID I DO?
YOU FORGOT TO WARN HIM ABOUT THE *BAD GIRLS!*
OOPS!

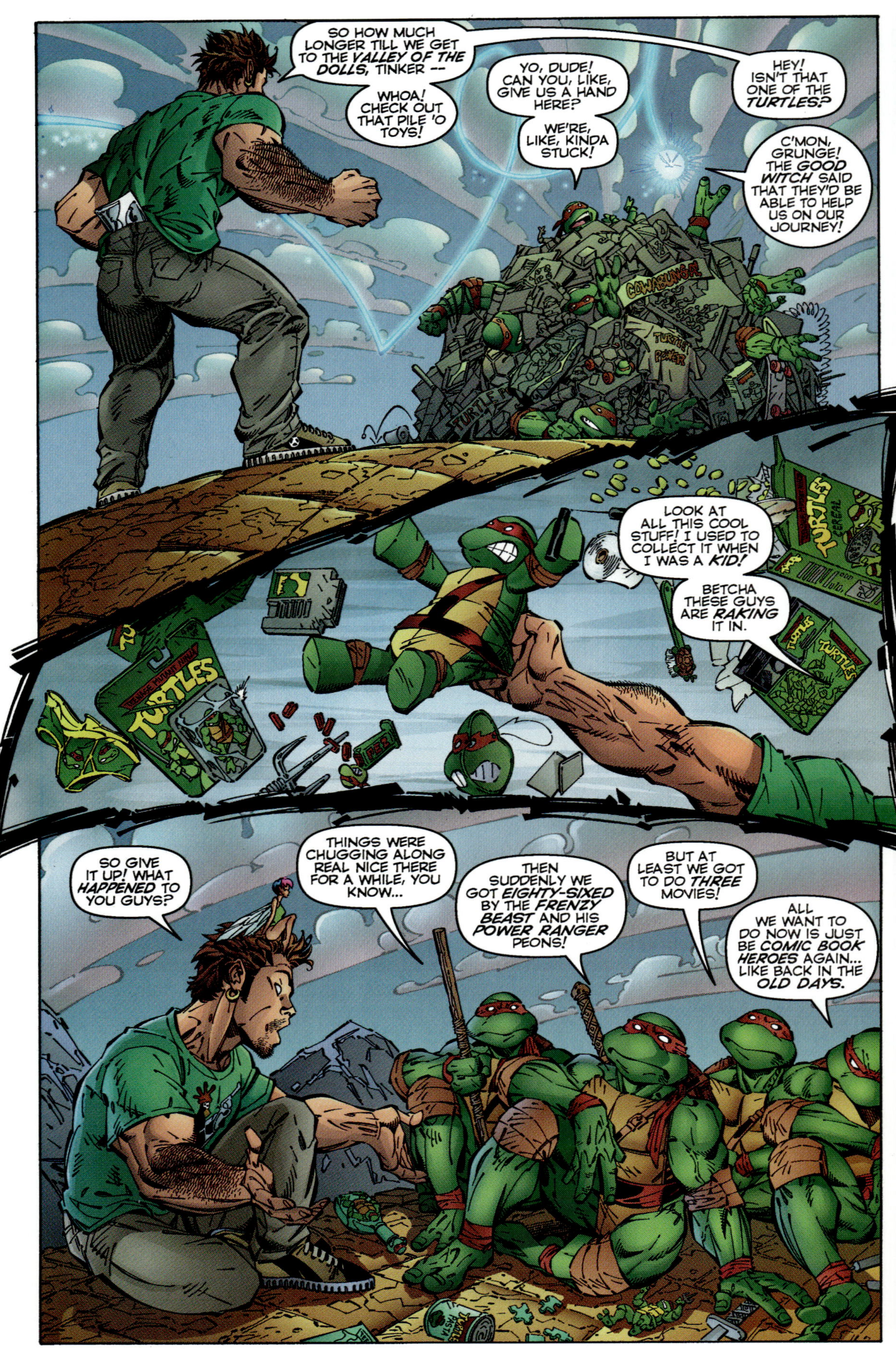
SO HOW MUCH LONGER TILL WE GET TO THE VALLEY OF THE DOLLS, TINKER --
WHOA! CHECK OUT THAT PILE 'O TOYS!
HEY! ISN'T THAT ONE OF THE TURTLES?
YO, DUDE! CAN YOU, LIKE, GIVE US A HAND HERE?
WE'RE, LIKE, KINDA STUCK!
C'MON, GRUNGE! THE GOOD WITCH SAID THAT THEY'D BE ABLE TO HELP US ON OUR JOURNEY!
COWABUNGA
TURTLE POWER
TURTLES CEREAL
LOOK AT ALL THIS COOL STUFF! I USED TO COLLECT IT WHEN I WAS A KID!
BETCHA THESE GUYS ARE RAKING IT IN.
TEENAGE MUTANT NINJA TURTLES
TURTLES
PEZ
SO GIVE IT UP! WHAT HAPPENED TO YOU GUYS?
THINGS WERE CHUGGING ALONG REAL NICE THERE FOR A WHILE, YOU KNOW...
THEN SUDDENLY WE GOT EIGHTY-SIXED BY THE FRENZY BEAST AND HIS POWER RANGER PEONS!
BUT AT LEAST WE GOT TO DO THREE MOVIES!
ALL WE WANT TO DO NOW IS JUST BE COMIC BOOK HEROES AGAIN... LIKE BACK IN THE OLD DAYS.

THANKS FOR DIGGING US OUT OF THE WRECKAGE, DUDE. ANYTHING WE CAN DO FOR YOU?
YOU WOULDN'T KNOW HOW TO GET TO THE VALLEY OF THE DOLLS, WOULD YOU?
THWACK
OOWWW! ALL RIGHT! ALL RIGHT!
ACTUALLY, WE'RE TRYING TO FIND THE WIZARD!
NO PROBLEMO, MAN.
JUST FOLLOW THE BEAST'S PATH OF DESTRUCTION.
WORD IS, THE WIZARD'S GOING AFTER HIM IN A BIG WAY.
IT OUGHTA TAKE YOU RIGHT TO 'EM!
WELL, PARTING IS SUCH SWEET SORROW, GUYS, BUT WE'RE OFF TO SEE THE WIZARD!
LOOK AT THAT! THE FRENZY BEAST MUST BE GETTING MORE POWERFUL EVERY DAY!
IT'S DESTROYING MORE AND MORE OF THE LAND OF S.A. IN THE PROCESS!
BE CAREFUL WHEN YOU GET TO THE FREELANCE FOREST! LOTS OF SCARY THINGS IN THERE!

DEEP INSIDE THE SCARY FOREST.

MMMM! *BONE* WILL MAKE A TASTY TREAT!

UH, GUYS, I HOPE YOU DIDN'T TAKE IT **PERSONALLY** WHEN I SAID THAT **RAT CREATURES** WERE **STUPID.**

TAKE A LOOK AT THIS, TINK! WHAT'S GOING ON OVER THERE?

IT'S A PAIR OF THE EVIL RAT CREATURES*!* THEY'RE MINIONS OF THE FRENZY BEAST!

UH-OH! LOOKS LIKE THEY'RE ABOUT TO TURN *DOUGH-BOY* OVER THERE INTO A *BISCUIT!*

HEY! THAT'S MY FRIEND, *FONE BONE!* WE'VE GOT TO SAVE HIM!

ZZZMMMMM

HUH?! ARE YOU LOCO?! THOSE RAT THINGS ARE *HUGE!*

HOLD ON, FONE! I'LL HAVE YOU OUT IN A JIFFY!
JUST KEEP AN EYE ON THE RAT CREATURE!
OH, I DON'T THINK WE'LL HAVE TO WORRY ABOUT HIM.
WHAM
MUST FIND HEL-- UNNGH!

YOWWCH! THAT %$#@ HURT! I DON'T GET IT!
I WAS HOLDING THIS PIECE OF ROCK WHEN I PUNCHED THAT THING, BUT MY HAND DIDN'T CHANGE. WHAT'S UP WITH MY GEN-FACTOR POWERS?!

OOPS! I KNEW THERE WAS SOMETHING I FORGOT TO TELL YOU.
GREAT! NOW YOU TELL ME THIS?! WHAT ELSE SHOULD I KNOW ABOUT?
WELL, I'D SUGGEST WE LEAVE BEFORE THESE TWO WAKE UP. SO WHERE ARE YOU GUYS GOING?

WE'RE LOOKING FOR THE WIZARD. SOME FRIENDS TOLD US THAT WE MIGHT FIND HIM IN THE VALLEY.
I'M HEADED THAT WAY MYSELF. WOULD YOU MIND SOME COMPANY?
IF YOU'RE COOL WITH TINK, YOU'RE COOL WITH ME. MAN, WHAT A LONG, STRANGE TRIP THIS HAS BEEN...

IN NEARBY BEANWORLD.
RIGHT YOU ARE, MR. SPOOK! IT'S CHOWDOWN TIME!
LET'S CELEBRATE OUR SUCCESSFUL RAID, CHOW SOL'JERS!
TIME FOR A SOAK IN THE CHOWDOWN POOL!

ARE WE EVER GOING TO GET THERE?! THIS TRIP IS TAKING LONGER TO FINISH THAN THAT FIRE FROM HEAVEN %$#@!
I'M FEELIN' HUNGRY AGAIN.
SO WHAT ELSE IS NEW?
WE CAN REST HERE FOR A LITTLE WHILE IF YOU LIKE. THE VALLEY ISN'T THAT MUCH FURTHER AWAY.
CHECK OUT THE WATER FOUNTAIN!
AT LEAST I CAN GET SOME LIQUID REFRESHMENT!

ACES! THERE ARE SOME TASTY LOOKING BEANS IN HERE TOO.
WATCH OUT, EVERYONE! WE'RE UNDER ATTACK!

AHHH! THIS OUGHTA HIT THE SPOT!
WE'RE ABOUT TO GET CHOWED!

HMMM. KINDA... CHEWY.
HELP!
OUCH!
?

CHOMP
CHOMP
CHOMP
GRUNGE! I DON'T THINK THOSE WERE ORDINARY BEANS!
SHE'S RIGHT! THOSE ARE LITTLE BEAN PEOPLE.
WE MUST BE IN BEANWORLD!

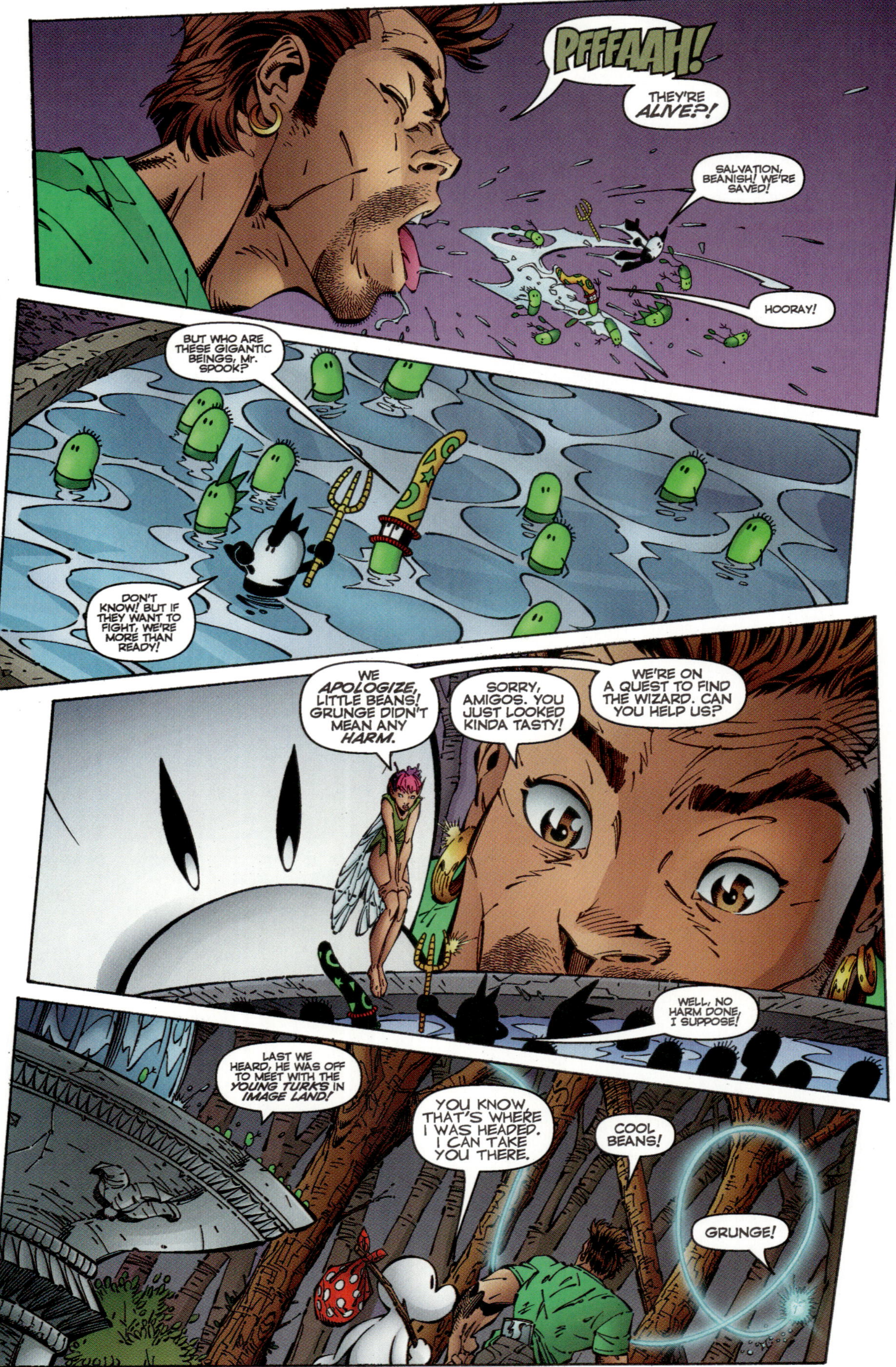
PFFFAAH!
THEY'RE ALIVE?!
SALVATION, BEANISH! WE'RE SAVED!
HOORAY!
BUT WHO ARE THESE GIGANTIC BEINGS, Mr. SPOOK?
DON'T KNOW! BUT IF THEY WANT TO FIGHT, WE'RE MORE THAN READY!
WE APOLOGIZE, LITTLE BEANS! GRUNGE DIDN'T MEAN ANY HARM.
SORRY, AMIGOS. YOU JUST LOOKED KINDA TASTY!
WE'RE ON A QUEST TO FIND THE WIZARD. CAN YOU HELP US?
WELL, NO HARM DONE, I SUPPOSE!
LAST WE HEARD, HE WAS OFF TO MEET WITH THE YOUNG TURKS IN IMAGE LAND!
YOU KNOW, THAT'S WHERE I WAS HEADED. I CAN TAKE YOU THERE.
COOL BEANS!
GRUNGE!

WOW! WOULD YOU LOOK AT THAT!
IT LOOKS LIKE THESE GUYS HAVE STARTED UP THEIR OWN INDEPENDENT COUNTRY. SO WHAT BRINGS YOU HERE, BONE-MAN?
WITH THE FRENZY BEAST RUNNING RAMPANT AROUND THE COUNTRYSIDE, I'M LOOKINGFOR A PLACE TO CHILL.
THESE YOUNG TURKS SEEM TO BEDOING A PRETTY GOOD JOB OF TAKING CARE OF THEMSELVES.

IMAGE-LAND
GEEZ, THE WIZARD COULD BE IN ANY ONE OF THESE VILLAGES, TINK!
I GUESS THAT MEANS WE'LL JUST HAVE TO CHECK THEM ALL OUT!

THIS IS WHERE I SAY GOODBYE. I'M GOING INTO TOWN TO PICK UP SOME SUPPLIES.
IMAGE-TOWN
HOPE YOU TWO FIND WHAT YOU'RE LOOKING FOR.
ASTRO
HIGHBROW CLUB
I TOLD YOU GUYS FOR THE LAST TIME!
YOU GOTTA HAVE A SENSE OF HUMOR IF YOU WANT TO FIT IN AROUND HERE!
WHO DO YOU SUPPOSE THAT GUY IS?
DON'T KNOW. HE DIDN'T GIVE HIS NAME.

TOP COW
I DON'T THINK THE WIZARD'S AROUND HERE EITHER. THIS PLACE LOOKS DESERTED.
BUT WHAT'S THE STORY WITH ALL THIS SPILT MILK?
RELOCATED!
THEY CAN'T DO THIS TO US!
HEY WHAT'S WITH THE RUCKUS OVER THERE?
NOTICE OF EVICTION
THEY'VE PUT A LIEN ON OUR BLOOD-QUARTERS?!
THEY CAN'T DO THAT TO US, CAPTAIN AVENGER!
BOOM
THAT AIN'T THE HALF OF IT, BLACK FRAG!
THE OTHER YOUNG TURKS! THEY -- THEY'VE KICKED US OUT OF IMAGE-LAND!
UH, PARDON ME, GUYS. BUT CAN YOU TELL ME WHERE I CAN FIND THE WIZARD?
THE WIZARD! I BET HE'S OVER AT THE WILDSTORM KEEP AGAIN! HE'S ALWAYS HANGING OUT THERE!
BLACK FRAG
THIS IS SO EXTREME!
THEY CAN'T DO THIS TO US!
UH, IF YOU ASK ME, I THINK THEY'VE ALREADY LOWERED THE BOOM.
SEEYA!

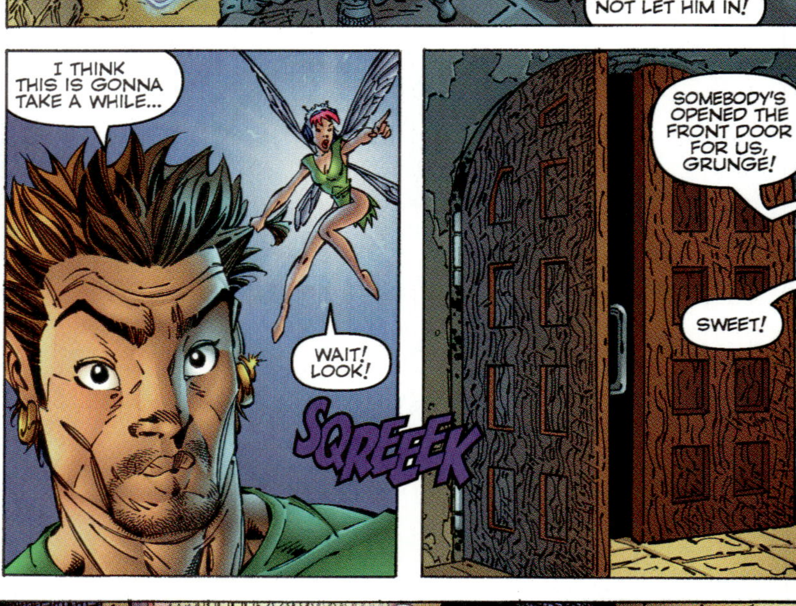

WOULD YOU LOOK AT THIS PLACE?

MAYBE THIS *Dr. FRANKENLYNCH* IS THE *WIZARD.*

NOBODY'S EVER REALLY SURE ABOUT WHAT'S GOING ON AROUND HERE!

GRUNGE! WATCH OUT!

LOOK! IT'S A *GROWN-UP!*

ARE YOU OUR *DADDY?!*

COME AGAIN?!
ACTUALLY, I'M JUST HERE TO LOOK FOR THE WIZARD.
Dr. FRANKENLYNCH IS THE ONLY ONE WHO CAN HELP YOU WITH THAT.
BUT HOLMES IS TOTALLY OFF HIS ROCKER.
HE'S BEEN LOCKED UP IN THE TOWER RE-SUS-CI-TATING THE OLD M-MONSTER!
ALL WE EVER DO IS LOOK FOR OUR PARENTS, WHO WERE FORCED TO ABANDON US WHEN WE WERE BABIES.
SO ARE YOU OUR DADDY?
UH, SORRY KID. DON'T THINK SO.
C'MON, GRUNGE! LET'S GET GOING!
TAKE IT EASY, TINK. THIS PLACE KINDA GIVES ME THE CREEPS.
OMIGOSH!
SOMEHOW, I DON'T THINK THIS IS THE GUY WE'RE LOOKING FOR.
THEY ALL SAID I WAS CRAZY! BUT I'LL SHOW THEM! WON'T I, LEEGOR? WITH A SIMPLE PULL OF THE SWITCH, I SHALL BRING THE M-MONSTER BACK TO LIFE!
OH! YES Dr. FRANKENLYNCH! YOU'LL SHOW THEM ALL!
SIMPLE PULL OF THE SWITCH, MY @$$! I DO ALL THE REAL WORK AROUND HERE BUT FRANKENLYNCH AND THOSE DAMN KIDS GET ALL THE CREDIT!
ZZRAPTT

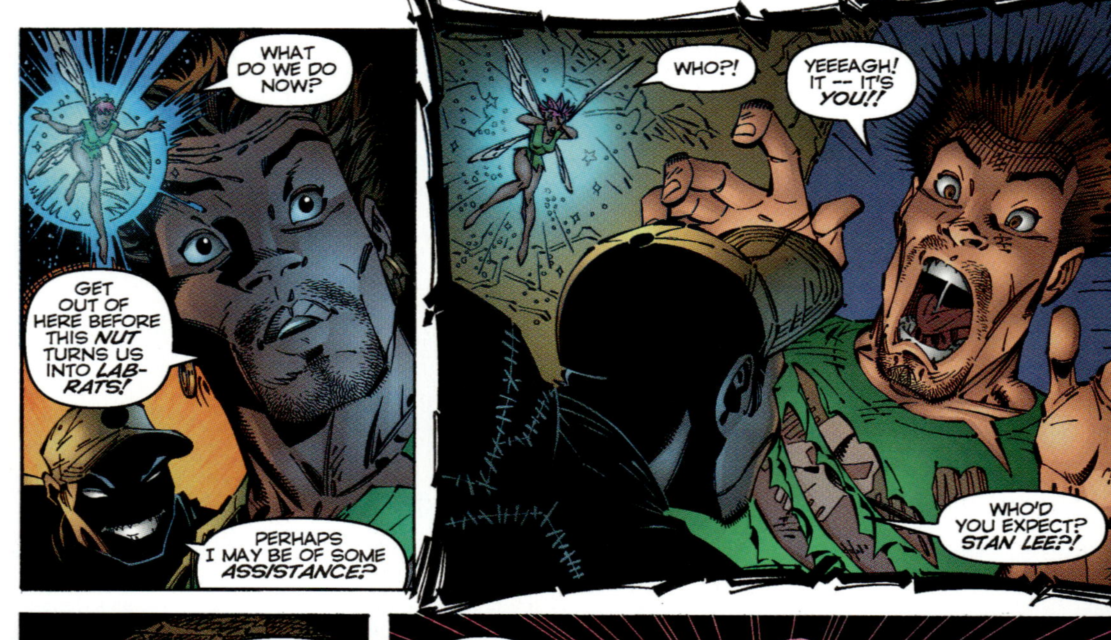
WHAT DO WE DO NOW?
GET OUT OF HERE BEFORE THIS NUT TURNS US INTO LAB-RATS!
PERHAPS I MAY BE OF SOME ASSISTANCE?
WHO?!
YEEEAGH! IT -- IT'S YOU!!
WHO'D YOU EXPECT? STAN LEE?!

HOW -- HOW'D YOU KNOW WE WERE HERE?
I KNOW EVERYTHING THAT GOES ON AROUND HERE! IF YOU HAVEN'T FIGURED IT OUT, THE WIZARD'S ALREADY LEFT TO GO BATTLE THE FRENZY BEAST.
NOW, FOLLOW ME. I'LL SET YOU IN THE RIGHT DIRECTION. YOU TWO ARE GOING TO NEED ALL THE HELP YOU CAN GET.

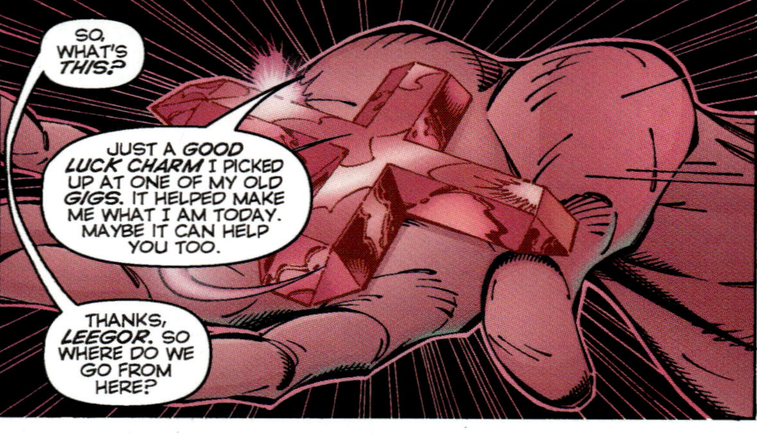
SO, WHAT'S THIS?
JUST A GOOD LUCK CHARM I PICKED UP AT ONE OF MY OLD GIGS. IT HELPED MAKE ME WHAT I AM TODAY. MAYBE IT CAN HELP YOU TOO.
THANKS, LEEGOR. SO WHERE DO WE GO FROM HERE?

YOU'LL FIND THE ANSWERS YOU SEEK IN THE ALLEYWAY!
NOW GO! BEFORE IT'S TOO LATE!
ENOUGH ALREADY WITH THE KUNG-FU GRASSHOPPER SPIEL! YOU GUYS NEED TO GO TALK TO SPAWN. HE'LL TELL YOU WHAT YOU WANT TO KNOW.
AND WATCH IT WITH THE HANDS THERE, BUDDY!

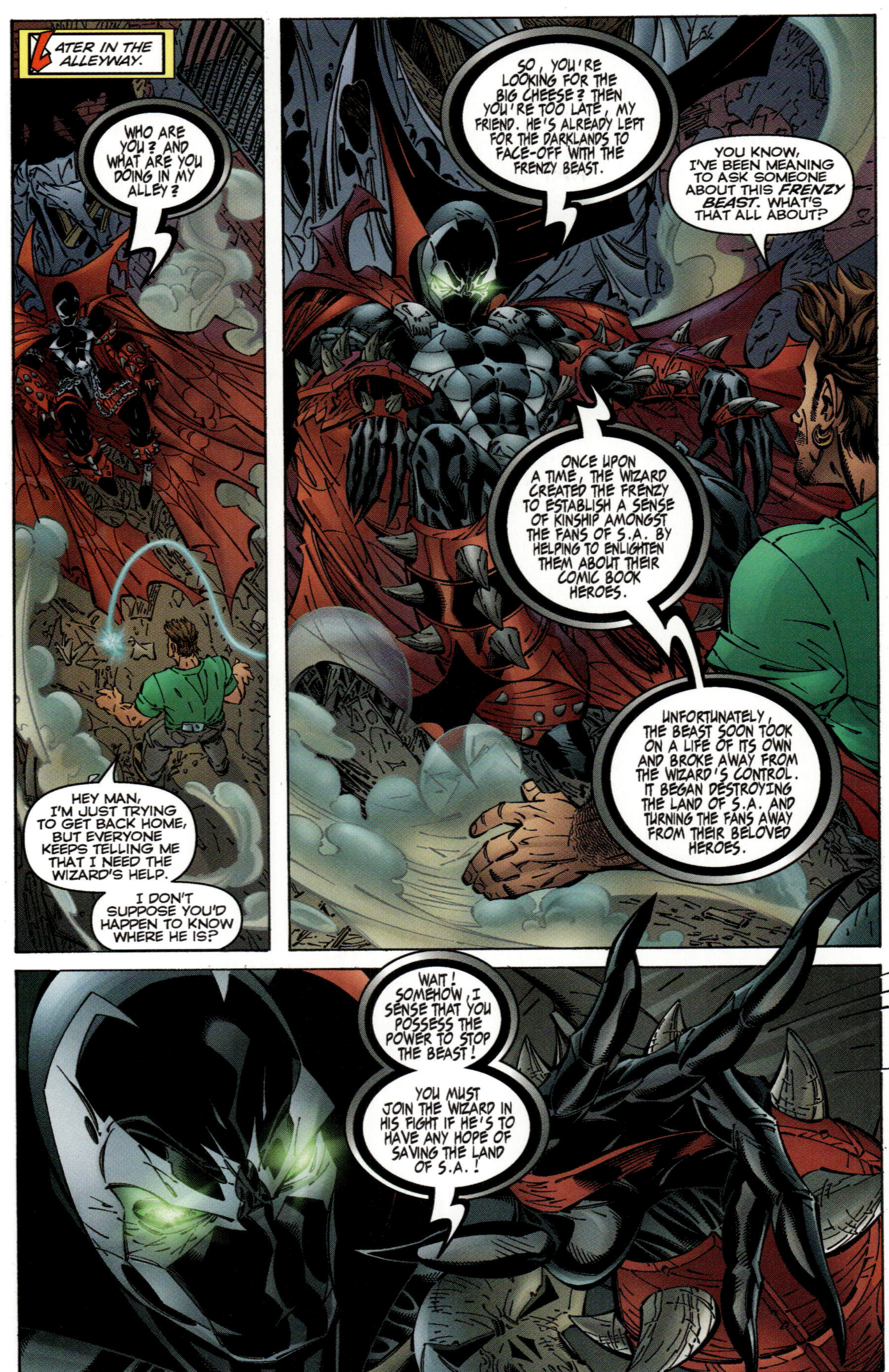
LATER IN THE ALLEYWAY.
WHO ARE YOU? AND WHAT ARE YOU DOING IN MY ALLEY?
HEY MAN, I'M JUST TRYING TO GET BACK HOME, BUT EVERYONE KEEPS TELLING ME THAT I NEED THE WIZARD'S HELP.
I DON'T SUPPOSE YOU'D HAPPEN TO KNOW WHERE HE IS?
SO, YOU'RE LOOKING FOR THE BIG CHEESE? THEN YOU'RE TOO LATE, MY FRIEND. HE'S ALREADY LEFT FOR THE DARKLANDS TO FACE-OFF WITH THE FRENZY BEAST.
YOU KNOW, I'VE BEEN MEANING TO ASK SOMEONE ABOUT THIS FRENZY BEAST. WHAT'S THAT ALL ABOUT?
ONCE UPON A TIME, THE WIZARD CREATED THE FRENZY TO ESTABLISH A SENSE OF KINSHIP AMONGST THE FANS OF S.A. BY HELPING TO ENLIGHTEN THEM ABOUT THEIR COMIC BOOK HEROES.
UNFORTUNATELY, THE BEAST SOON TOOK ON A LIFE OF ITS OWN AND BROKE AWAY FROM THE WIZARD'S CONTROL. IT BEGAN DESTROYING THE LAND OF S.A. AND TURNING THE FANS AWAY FROM THEIR BELOVED HEROES.
WAIT! SOMEHOW, I SENSE THAT YOU POSSESS THE POWER TO STOP THE BEAST!
YOU MUST JOIN THE WIZARD IN HIS FIGHT IF HE'S TO HAVE ANY HOPE OF SAVING THE LAND OF S.A.!

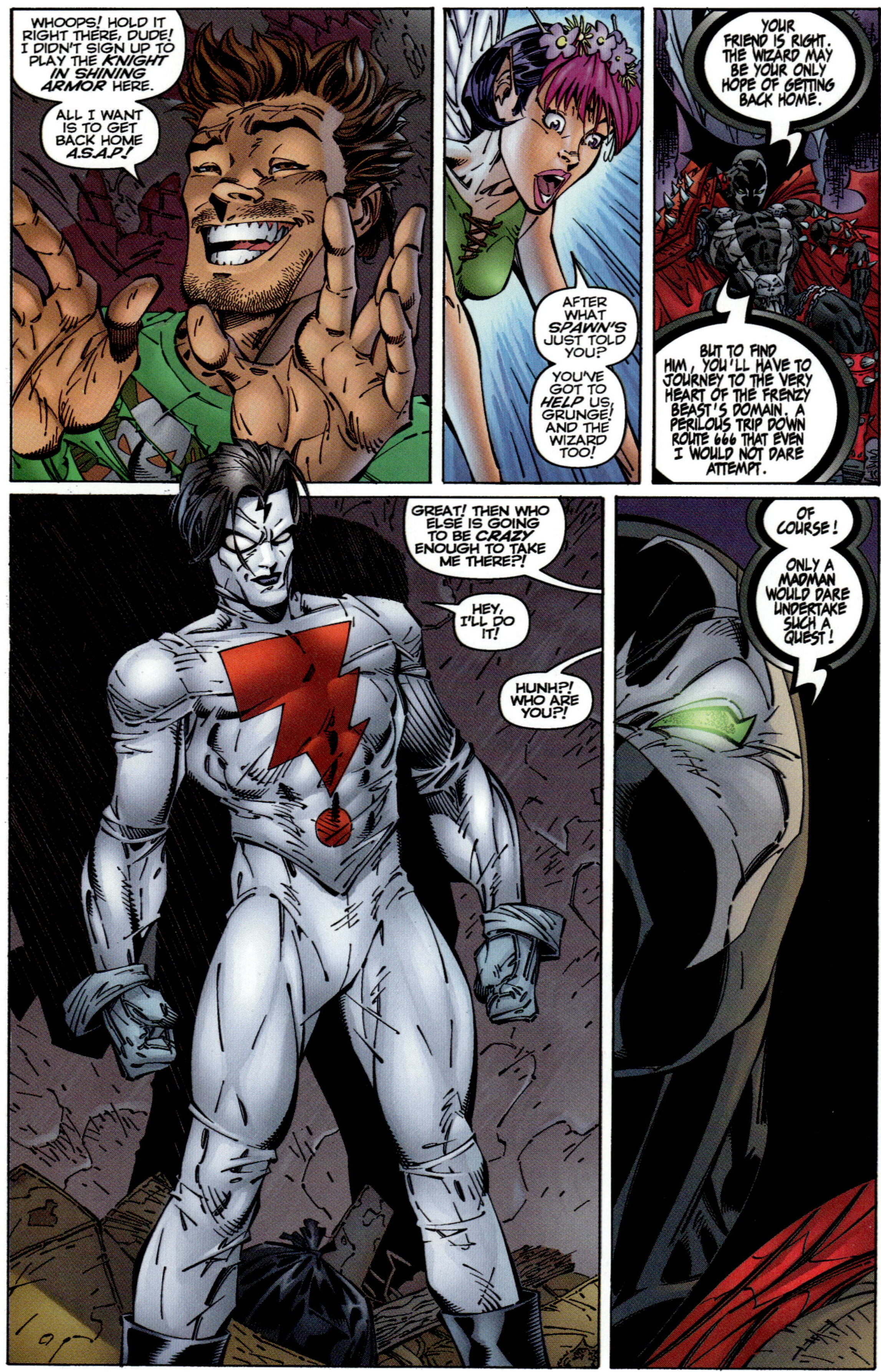
WHOOPS! HOLD IT RIGHT THERE, DUDE! I DIDN'T SIGN UP TO PLAY THE KNIGHT IN SHINING ARMOR HERE.
ALL I WANT IS TO GET BACK HOME A.S.A.P.!
AFTER WHAT SPAWN'S JUST TOLD YOU?
YOU'VE GOT TO HELP US, GRUNGE! AND THE WIZARD TOO!
YOUR FRIEND IS RIGHT. THE WIZARD MAY BE YOUR ONLY HOPE OF GETTING BACK HOME.
BUT TO FIND HIM, YOU'LL HAVE TO JOURNEY TO THE VERY HEART OF THE FRENZY BEAST'S DOMAIN. A PERILOUS TRIP DOWN ROUTE 666 THAT EVEN I WOULD NOT DARE ATTEMPT.
GREAT! THEN WHO ELSE IS GOING TO BE CRAZY ENOUGH TO TAKE ME THERE?!
HEY, I'LL DO IT!
HUNH?! WHO ARE YOU?!
OF COURSE!
ONLY A MADMAN WOULD DARE UNDERTAKE SUCH A QUEST!

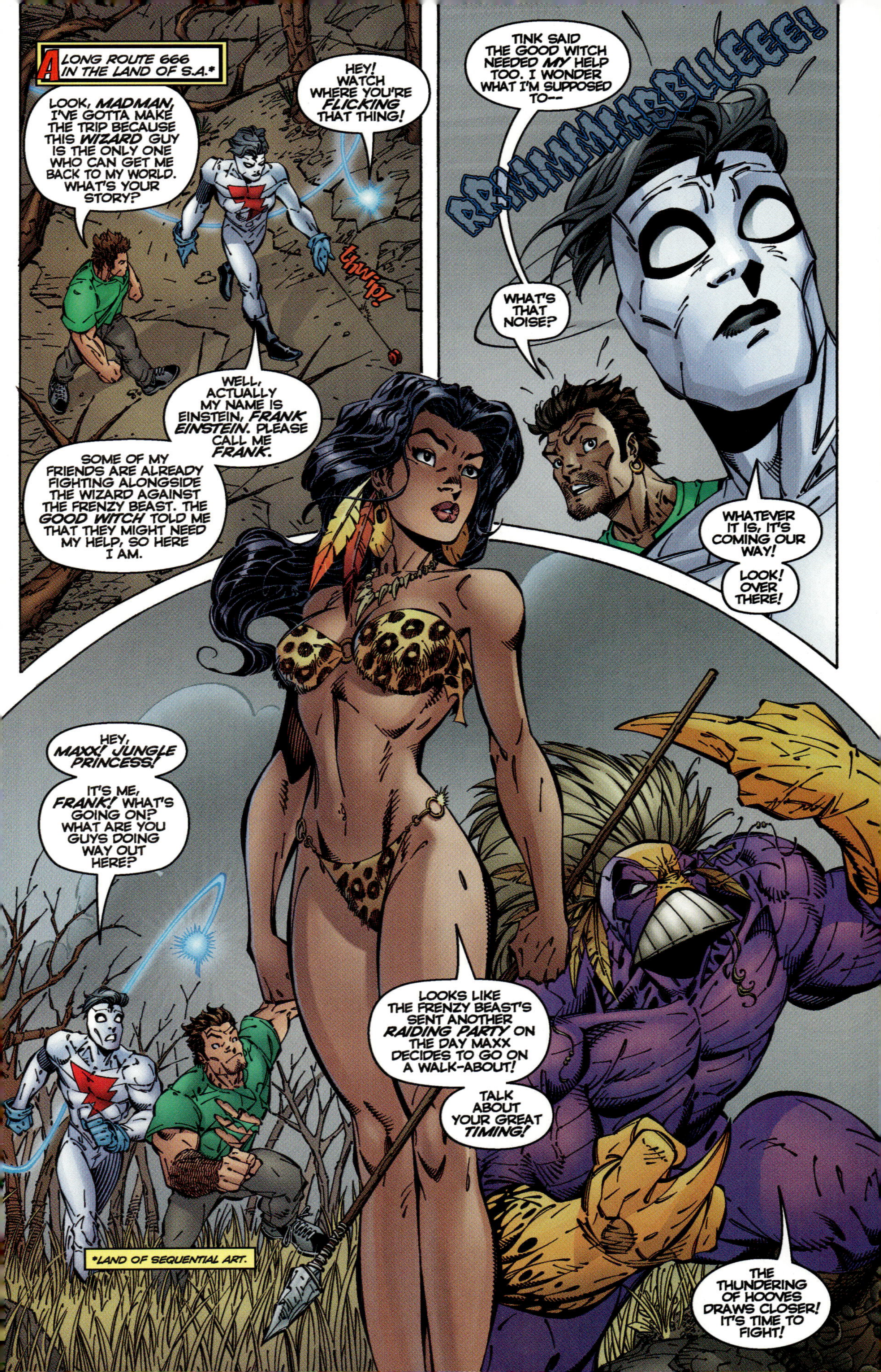
ALONG ROUTE 666 IN THE LAND OF S.A.*
LOOK, MADMAN, I'VE GOTTA MAKE THE TRIP BECAUSE THIS WIZARD GUY IS THE ONLY ONE WHO CAN GET ME BACK TO MY WORLD. WHAT'S YOUR STORY?
HEY! WATCH WHERE YOU'RE FLICKING THAT THING!
THWIP!
WELL, ACTUALLY MY NAME IS EINSTEIN, FRANK EINSTEIN. PLEASE CALL ME FRANK.
SOME OF MY FRIENDS ARE ALREADY FIGHTING ALONGSIDE THE WIZARD AGAINST THE FRENZY BEAST. THE GOOD WITCH TOLD ME THAT THEY MIGHT NEED MY HELP, SO HERE I AM.
TINK SAID THE GOOD WITCH NEEDED MY HELP TOO. I WONDER WHAT I'M SUPPOSED TO--
BRRMMMMBLLGGG!
WHAT'S THAT NOISE?
WHATEVER IT IS, IT'S COMING OUR WAY!
LOOK! OVER THERE!
HEY, MAXX! JUNGLE PRINCESS!
IT'S ME, FRANK! WHAT'S GOING ON? WHAT ARE YOU GUYS DOING WAY OUT HERE?
LOOKS LIKE THE FRENZY BEAST'S SENT ANOTHER RAIDING PARTY ON THE DAY MAXX DECIDES TO GO ON A WALK-ABOUT!
TALK ABOUT YOUR GREAT TIMING!
THE THUNDERING OF HOOVES DRAWS CLOSER! IT'S TIME TO FIGHT!
*LAND OF SEQUENTIAL ART.

UH-OH, MAXX! IT LOOKS AS THOUGH THE FRENZY BEAST HAS SENT THE *BAD GIRLS!*

THERE HE IS! THE ONE THAT OUR MASTER SEEKS!

CAN WE JUST GET THIS OVER WITH?! I'M GOING TO *CATCH A COLD* WEARING THIS OUTFIT!

STOMP! STOMP! STOMP

MISOGYNISTIC DOG! OFF WITH YOUR HEAD--
KA-TANG
SORRY. WERE YOU TALKING TO ME?
WHO DARES TO CROSS SWORDS WITH LADY MORTEM?!
YEAH! WHO DARES?
FIVE MINUTES! THAT'S ALL I ASK FOR! FIVE MORE MINUTES!
SORRY, FRIEND, BUT IT IS OUR DUTY TO PROTECT YOU.
DO NOT LET LADY MORTEM SEDUCE YOU WITH HER SECRET CHARMS!
EXCUSE ME, GIVE ME A BREAK!
THAT BIMBO'S GOT ENOUGH PLASTIC IN HER CHEST TO START A BARBIE DOLL FACTORY!
LISTEN UP, LADY MORTEM. YOUR THREE HORSES AREN'T GOING TO DO MUCH GOOD AGAINST THE THREE HUNDRED AND FIFTY HORSES THAT KATCHOO AND I HAVE UNDER THIS HOOD.
SO WHY DON'T YOU LIKE, RETREAT, OR SOMETHING?!
OH, THAT'S TELLING HER, FRANCINE. I THINK I SAW HER LIP QUIVER!
HEY, SHI-RA! YOU WANNA CHILL ON THE HOOD ORNAMENT BIT?!

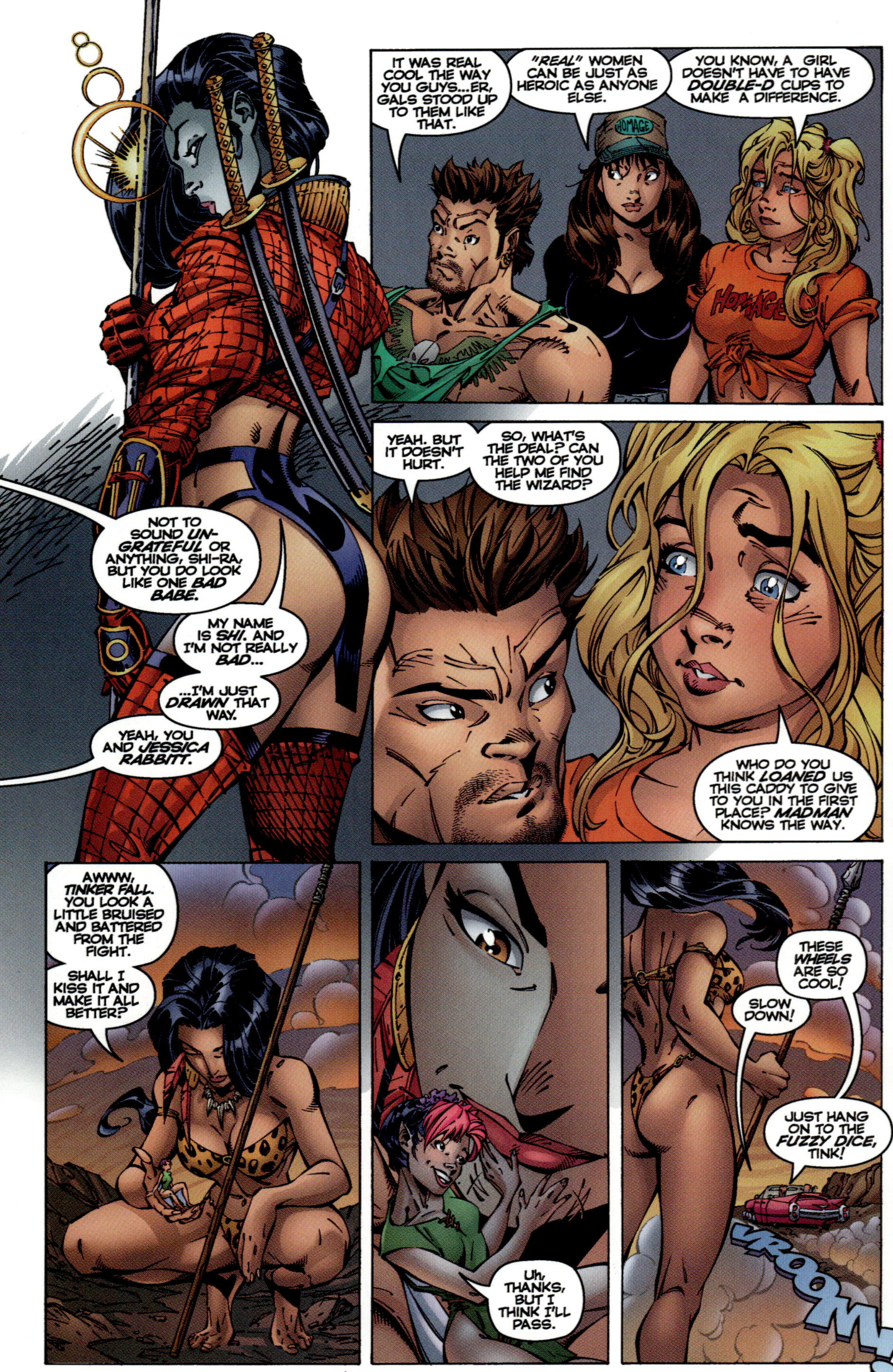
IT WAS REAL COOL THE WAY YOU GUYS...ER, GALS STOOD UP TO THEM LIKE THAT.
"REAL" WOMEN CAN BE JUST AS HEROIC AS ANYONE ELSE.
YOU KNOW, A GIRL DOESN'T HAVE TO HAVE DOUBLE-D CUPS TO MAKE A DIFFERENCE.
HOMAGE
HOMAGE
NOT TO SOUND UN-GRATEFUL OR ANYTHING, SHI-RA, BUT YOU DO LOOK LIKE ONE BAD BABE.
MY NAME IS SHI. AND I'M NOT REALLY BAD...
...I'M JUST DRAWN THAT WAY.
YEAH, YOU AND JESSICA RABBITT.
YEAH. BUT IT DOESN'T HURT.
SO, WHAT'S THE DEAL? CAN THE TWO OF YOU HELP ME FIND THE WIZARD?
WHO DO YOU THINK LOANED US THIS CADDY TO GIVE TO YOU IN THE FIRST PLACE? MADMAN KNOWS THE WAY.
AWWW, TINKER FALL. YOU LOOK A LITTLE BRUISED AND BATTERED FROM THE FIGHT.
SHALL I KISS IT AND MAKE IT ALL BETTER?
Uh, THANKS, BUT I THINK I'LL PASS.
THESE WHEELS ARE SO COOL!
SLOW DOWN!
JUST HANG ON TO THE FUZZY DICE, TINK!
VROOOM!

MEANWHILE, OUT NEAR THE FRONTIER.
MY FRIENDS, OUR SITUATION IS DIRE INDEED!
IT WOULD APPEAR THAT THE FRENZY BEAST IS PREPARING TO LAUNCH A FINAL ASSAULT AGAINST THE LAND OF S.A.!
I'M WORRIED ABOUT THE WIZARD, AXWELL. HE SHOULD'VE BEEN BACK BY NOW.
...
HELLBOY, DO YOU THINK WE'LL BE ABLE TO HOLD OFF THE BEAST?
DOESN'T LOOK TOO GOOD, ANN.
THE WIZARD SHOULDN'T HAVE GONE AFTER THAT THING ALONE! WE NEED TO STICK TOGETHER.
IT'S GONNA TAKE A MIRACLE TO SAVE US NOW!
VRROOOOM!
'SUP, DUDES! ANYBODY SEE A WIZARD AROUND THESE PARTS?
SREECH!
HAVE NO FEAR, THE CAVALRY IS HERE!
ANN! HELLBOY! MADMAN HAS ARRIVED!

GUYS, MEET GRUNGE. HE'S THE SOLUTION TO OUR PROBLEM! HE HAS THE CHROMIUM COVER!
Huh? WHAT'S MY COMIC BOOK GOT TO DO WITH ANY-THING?!
SO YOU'RE THE ONE THE FRENZY BEAST IS AFTER!
THAT MEANS YOU'RE THE KEY TO STOPPING HIM! BUT FIRST WE JUST HAVE TO FIGURE OUT HOW!
WWWHHHOOOOOSSSHH!
UNFORTUNATELY, ANN, IT APPEARS THAT WE'VE RUN OUT OF TIME!
STRIKE! HOLD UP, CRAZY CATS. I AIN'T STANDING IN THE WAY OF SOME FRENZY TWISTER! YOU THINK THIS IS SOME KINDA MOVIE?
ARE YOU GUYS INSANE?!
HEY, I'M UP FOR IT!
THIS IS IT GUYS, ALAMO TIME!
GEE! NOW, THERE'S A SURPRISE!
BEAST, YOU MUST LISTEN TO ME! STOP THIS MAD-NESS!
BY KILLING THESE HEROES, YOU'LL ONLY BE DESTROYING YOURSELF!
YOUR WARNINGS DON'T FRIGHTEN ME, WIZARD!
SO, I SEE THAT SOME OF THE LEGENDS OF S.A. HAVE JOINED FORCES TO TRY AND STOP ME!
FOOLS! SELL ME YOUR SOULS AND I MIGHT LET YOU LIVE!
WE'D RATHER DIE!
REMEMBER! THE KEY TO DEFEATING HIM IS THE CHROMIUM COVER!
BUT WHAT AM I SUPPOSED TO DO WITH IT?
AAAAHHH, YEESSS! I SENSE THAT THE TATTOOED DWARF POSSESSES THE PRIZE I SEEK!
GIVE IT TO ME AND YOU SHALL HAVE YOUR HEART'S DESIRE!
NO! DON'T LISTEN TO HIM! YOU MUST--
ENOUGH! IF YOU WON'T GIVE IT TO ME...

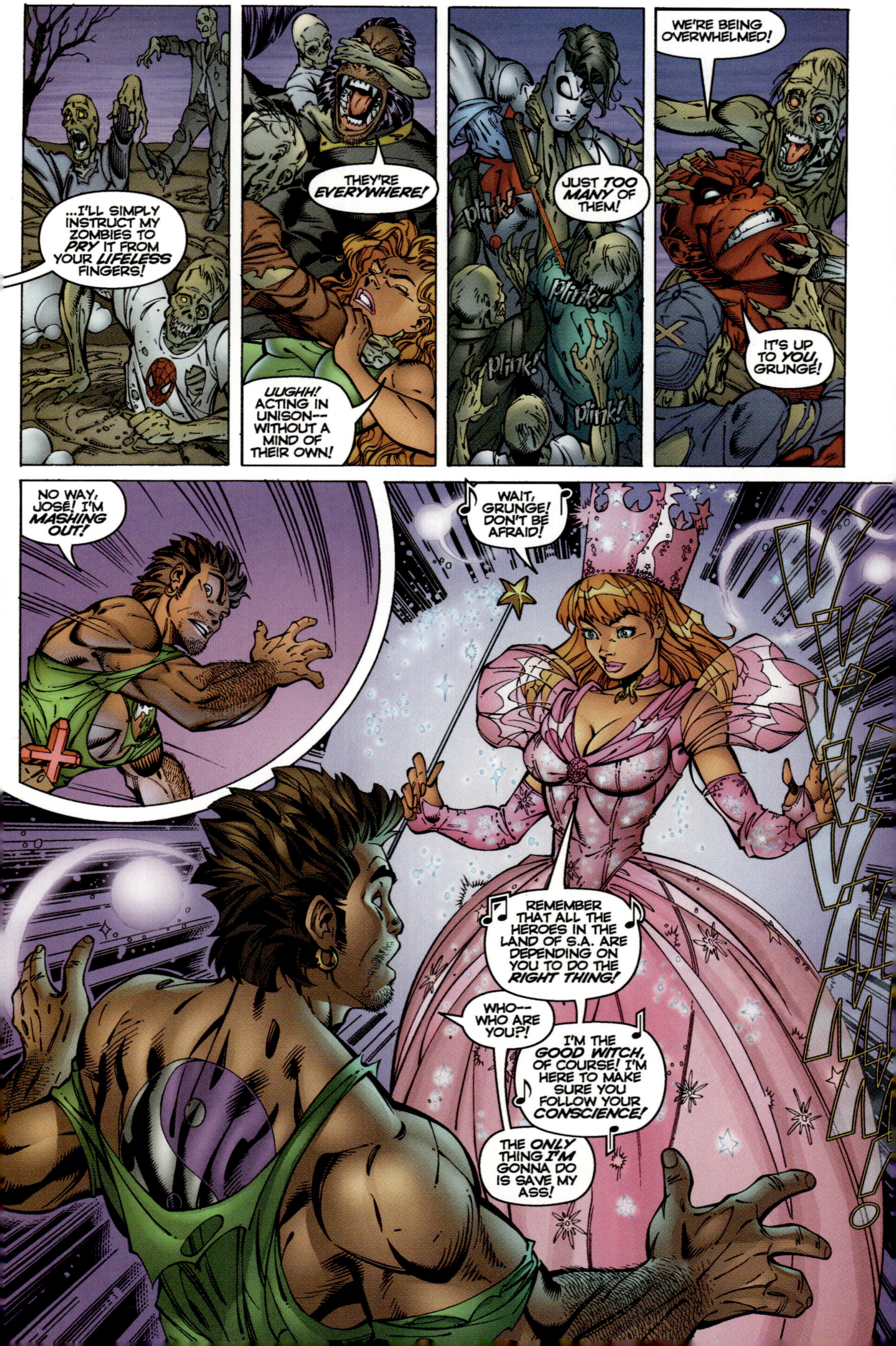

...I'LL SIMPLY INSTRUCT MY ZOMBIES TO *PRY* IT FROM YOUR *LIFELESS* FINGERS!

THEY'RE *EVERYWHERE!*
UUGHH! ACTING IN UNISON-- WITHOUT A MIND OF THEIR OWN!

JUST *TOO MANY* OF THEM!
plink!
plink!
plink!
plink!

WE'RE BEING OVERWHELMED!
IT'S UP TO *YOU,* GRUNGE!

NO WAY, JOSÉ! I'M *MASHING OUT!*
WAIT, GRUNGE! DON'T BE AFRAID!
REMEMBER THAT ALL THE HEROES IN THE LAND OF S.A. ARE DEPENDING ON YOU TO DO THE *RIGHT THING!*
WHO-- WHO ARE YOU?!
I'M THE *GOOD WITCH,* OF COURSE! I'M HERE TO MAKE SURE YOU FOLLOW YOUR *CONSCIENCE!*
THE *ONLY* THING *I'M* GONNA DO IS SAVE MY ASS!

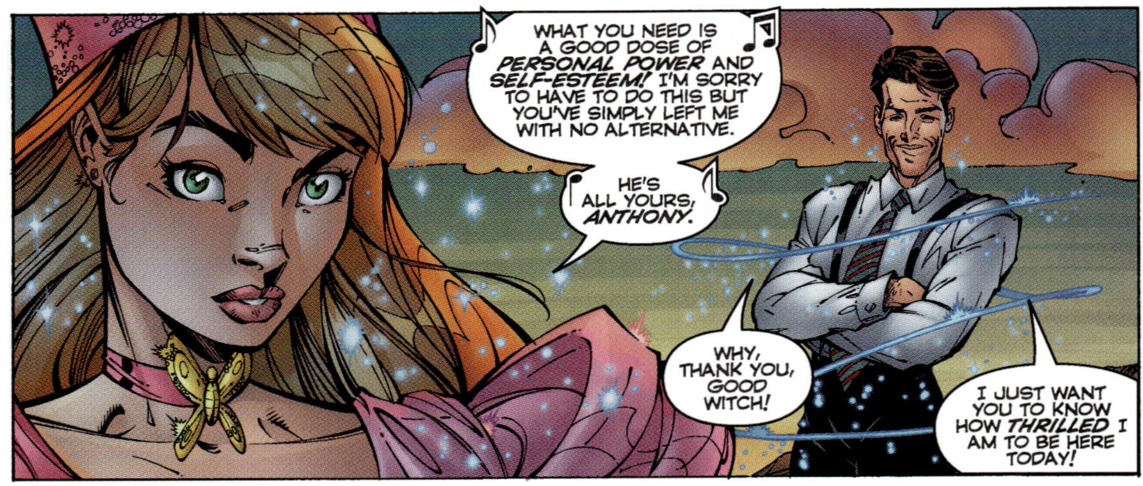
WHAT YOU NEED IS A GOOD DOSE OF PERSONAL POWER AND SELF-ESTEEM! I'M SORRY TO HAVE TO DO THIS BUT YOU'VE SIMPLY LEFT ME WITH NO ALTERNATIVE.
HE'S ALL YOURS, ANTHONY.
WHY, THANK YOU, GOOD WITCH!
I JUST WANT YOU TO KNOW HOW THRILLED I AM TO BE HERE TODAY!

YOU! YOU'RE THE DUDE IN ALL THOSE INFO-MERCIALS!
THAT'S RIGHT, GRUNGE! OVER THESE PAST FEW YEARS, I'VE HELPED MILLIONS TRANSFER THEIR LIVES WITH MY SPECIAL PERSONAL POWER PROGRAM--
--AND I CAN DO THE SAME FOR YOU!
REALLY?

YOU KNOW, I WAS A LOT LIKE YOU WHEN I WAS A KID...
...GOING NOWHERE WITH NOTHING TO MY NAME.
BUT ONE DAY, I CHANGED ALL THAT BY LEARNING TO MASTER MY LIFE AND TODAY I'M A SUCCESSFUL ENTREPRENEUR, RUNNING MY OWN MULTI-NATIONAL, MULTI-MILLION DOLLAR COR-PORATION!

BY FOLLOWING MY PASSION, I NOW DRIVE A FERRARI, LIVE IN A FABULOUS MANSION, AND HAVE THE LIFE OF MY DREAMS.
WOULDN'T YOU LIKE TO HAVE THIS QUALITY OF LIFE, TOO?
WHO WOULDN'T? BUT HOW?
OOO

BY UNLEASHING THE POWER WITHIN YOU AND AWAKENING THE GIANT INSIDE!
TAKE CONTROL OF YOUR LIFE, GRUNGE, AND HARNESS THE FORCES THAT SHAPE YOUR LIFE!
FOLLOW YOUR PASSION AND FORGE YOUR DESTINY!
YOU KNOW SOMETHING...

YOU'RE RIGHT, TONY!

THEN GET OUT THERE AND MAKE A DIFFERENCE, MY FRIEND!
I'LL DO IT!
EVEN IF THAT MEANS BATTLING A HORDE OF MIND-LESS ZOMBIES ALL BY MY-SELF!
WELL, GIVE IT YOUR BEST SHOT!
HUH?! LEEGOR'S AMULET IS STARTING TO GLOW!
ZZMMMM!
YA GOT HEART, KID! BUT YA BETTER LET ME TAKE CARE OF THEM!
VVVSSH
WHOA, CHECK IT OUT!
SNIKT!
'CAUSE AFTER ALL...
I'M THE BEST THERE IS AT WHAT I DO!
WHO ARE YOU, MASKED MAN?
JUST THINK OF ME AS A NEW FRIEND.
NOW, YA BETTER GET GOIN' AND FINISH THIS JOB!

LISTEN UP, FRENZY BEAST!
I DON'T KNOW WHAT YOUR GAME IS, BUT I'M HERE TO SHUT YOU DOWN!
CHILL, DUDE! WHY ALL THE HOSTILITY?
HEY! THAT'S MY FACE! GIVE IT BACK!
DON'T YOU SEE, GRUNGE? THE TWO OF US? WE'RE THE SAME. I ONLY WANT YOUR CHROMIUM COVER SO I CAN COMPLETE MY SET. SURELY YOU CAN UNDERSTAND THAT!
SO, HERE'S THE DEAL. GIVE ME THE LAST OF THE CHROMIUM COVERS AND IN EXCHANGE...
I'LL GIVE YOU THE FAME AND FORTUNE YOU'VE ALWAYS DREAMED OF AS A ROCK AND ROLL SUPERSTAR! JUST THINK, YOU'LL BE ABLE TO HAVE ANY WOMAN YOU DESIRE!
SAY, NOW! MY VERY OWN GROUPIES?!
DON'T LISTEN TO HIM, GRUNGE!
YOU'LL ONLY MAKE THE BEAST MORE POWER-FUL!
HE'LL TAKE OVER YOUR WORLD THE SAME WAY HE TOOK OVER THE LAND OF S.A.!
NO WAY, BEAST-MAN! I SEE YOU FOR WHAT YOU REALLY ARE!
I WON'T LET MY FRIENDS DOWN...AND YOU'LL NEVER GET THIS BOOK!

NO MINT COPY FOR YOU!
RRIIIP!
KRACKLE!
KA-BOOOM!
STOP, YOU FOOL! DO YOU HAVE ANY IDEA WHAT YOU'VE DONE?!
NOW YOU'LL *NEVER* GET HOME!
DO YOU *HEAR* ME?! NEEEVVVEEER!
AAAARRRGGH!
AT LEAST YOUR *COLLECTING DAYS* ARE OVER!
YEEEOOOW!

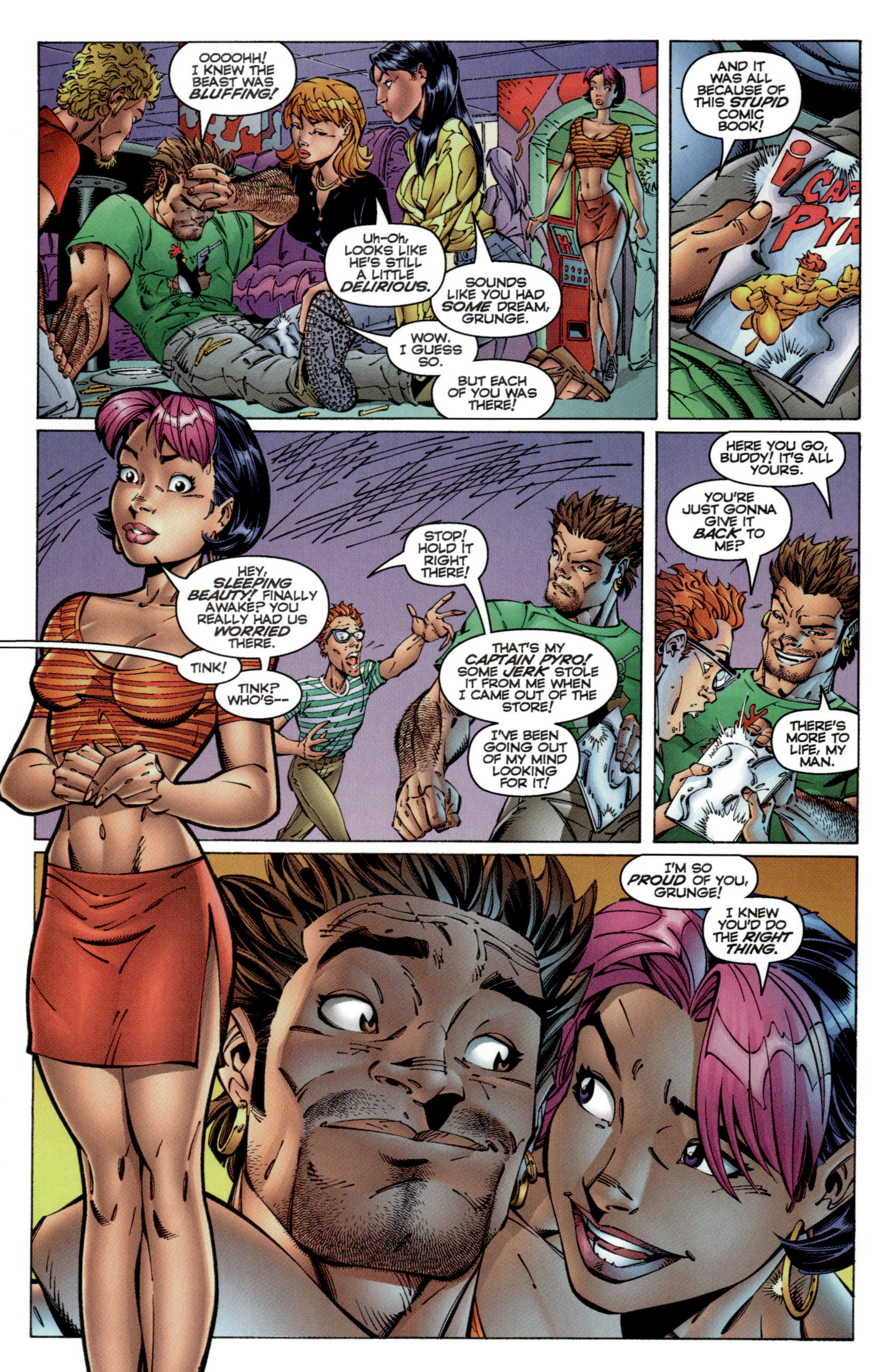
OOOOHH! I KNEW THE BEAST WAS BLUFFING!
Uh-Oh, LOOKS LIKE HE'S STILL A LITTLE DELIRIOUS.
SOUNDS LIKE YOU HAD SOME DREAM, GRUNGE.
WOW. I GUESS SO.
BUT EACH OF YOU WAS THERE!
AND IT WAS ALL BECAUSE OF THIS STUPID COMIC BOOK!
CAPTAIN PYRO
HEY, SLEEPING BEAUTY! FINALLY AWAKE? YOU REALLY HAD US WORRIED THERE.
TINK!
TINK? WHO'S--
STOP! HOLD IT RIGHT THERE!
THAT'S MY CAPTAIN PYRO! SOME JERK STOLE IT FROM ME WHEN I CAME OUT OF THE STORE!
I'VE BEEN GOING OUT OF MY MIND LOOKING FOR IT!
HERE YOU GO, BUDDY! IT'S ALL YOURS.
YOU'RE JUST GONNA GIVE IT BACK TO ME?
THERE'S MORE TO LIFE, MY MAN.
I'M SO PROUD OF YOU, GRUNGE!
I KNEW YOU'D DO THE RIGHT THING.

YOU'VE ALWAYS BEEN THERE FOR ME, HAVEN'T YOU, ROX?
BUT I'VE JUST BEEN TOO BLIND TO SEE IT!
Huh?!
WHAT'RE YOU DOING, GRUNGE?
SOMETHING THAT'S BEEN LONG OVER-DUE!
SMOOOOCH!
Mmmmmmm!
NOW I'VE SEEN EVERYTHING!
ACTUALLY, I WISH I HADN'T.
IF THE TWO OF YOU DON'T MIND, THE REST OF US WOULD LIKE TO KEEP OUR LUNCH DOWN.
LET'S GO HOME. WE BETTER GET OUT OF HERE BEFORE THEY "SHED THEIR THREADS."
DON'T MIND THEM, TINK. THEY'RE JUST JEALOUS!
EXCUSE ME? MY NAME'S ROXY?!
THAT'S ALL FOLKS!
AND THEY ALL LIVED...
... WELL, YOU'LL FIND OUT SOON ENOUGH!
The End

CREDITS

STORY: BRANDON CHOI, J. SCOTT CAMPBELL & JIM LEE

PENCILS: J. SCOTT CAMPBELL

INKS: ALEX GARNER
WITH RICHARD FRIEND, TOM MCWEENEY & EDWIN ROSELL

COLORS: JOE CHIODO & MARTIN JIMENEZ

INK ASSIST: PETER GUZMAN

LETTERS: BILL O'NEIL

COMPUTER COLORS: WILDSTORM FX

ORIGINAL SERIES ASSISTANT EDITOR: GIGI BARBES

ORIGINAL SERIES EDITOR: SARAH BECKER

COLLECTION EDITOR: SCOTT DUNBIER

COVER BY J. SCOTT CAMPBELL & SANDRA HOPE

GEN13 CREATED BY BRANDON CHOI, JIM LEE & J. SCOTT CAMPBELL

WS FX:
JOEL BENJAMIN, ALEX CARBONERO, LAURA DEPUY, BEN DIMAGMALIW, TAD EHRLICH, MICHAEL GARCIA, GUY MAJOR, JUSTIN PONSOR, DAVID RODRIGUEZ, DARLENE ROYER, JESSICA RUFFNER, CARLOS VASQUEZ & ANTHONY WASHINGTON

WS PRODUCTION:
HAFID BOULANOUAR, BONNIE BREMNER, RUTH CASTILLO, CLAUDIA CHONG, JENNIFER FENNER, AMIE GRENIER, SILBINA LEPE, TOM LONG, DENICE PARK, ROBERT PARTRIDGE, ROB ROBBINS, ED ROEDER, COREY WARD AND JAN ZACHARIAS

DESIGN:
EMILIO MEDINA

SARAH DITZER & THOM P. SULLIVAN: PRODUCTION MANAGERS

JOE COTRUPE: VICE PRESIDENT OF MANUFACTURING

JIM LEE: EDITOR IN CHIEF

LARRY MARDER: EXECUTIVE DIRECTOR OF IMAGE COMICS

Gen13 #13 A, B & C Collected Edition. November 1997. FIRST PRINTING. Image Comics, Inc. Office of Publication: 1440 N. Harbor Blvd., Suite 305, Fullerton, California 92835. Direct Market: $6.95/$10.10 in Canada.

Acknowledgments

WildStorm Productions wishes to thank the following people for their immeasurable help and generosity in making this book a reality.

Arthur Adams

Mike Allred

Nanci Dakesian

Kevin Eastman

Bob Harras

Sam Kieth

Peter Laird

Larry Marder

Todd McFarlane

Mike Mignola

Terry Moore

Gary Richardson

Anthony Robbins

Michael Silberkleit

Jeff Smith

Billy Tucci

ON THE NEXT FOUR PAGES WE PRESENT THE COVERS OF THE ORIGINAL SERIES, AS WELL AS THIS TRADE PAPERBACK, FREE OF THEIR LOGO AND DESIGN ELEMENTS.

COVER A IS BY J. SCOTT CAMPBELL & ALEX GARNER.

COVER B IS BY J. SCOTT CAMPBELL & ALEX GARNER, WITH A LITTLE HELP FROM JEFF SMITH, WHO HELPED THEM "BONE" UP ON A CERTAIN CHARACTER.

Cover C is by J. Scott Campbell & Alex Garner

THE TPB COVER IS BY J. SCOTT CAMPBELL & SANDRA HOPE

RANDOM THOUGHTS
ANTHONY ROBBINS:
WHILE CHALLENGING PEOPLE TO STEP UP AND SHAPE THEIR DESTINIES IN THE DIRECTION OF THEIR DREAMS IS WHAT I DO EVERY DAY OF MY LIFE, I NEVER THOUGHT I'D HAVE THE OPPORTUNITY TO BRING THIS MESSAGE TO THE VIRTUAL WORLD OF THE COMIC BOOK. GEN13 IS EXTRAORDINARY, AND I WAS THRILLED TO BE INCLUDED AS A CHARACTER.
ARCHIE:
ARCHIE ANDREWS IS CRAMMING FOR FINALS AND IS UNAVAILABLE FOR COMMENT.
MIKE MIGNOLA:
J. SCOTT CAMPBELL'S HELLBOY LOOKS ALL HEALTHY AND SHINY, UNLIKE THE BROKEN DOWN HEAP OF MISERY I DRAW.
ARTHUR ADAMS:
WITH MONKEY MAN & O'BRIEN'S APPEARANCE IN GEN13 #13, JEFF CAMPBELL HAS MANAGED TO DOUBLE THE ENTIRE MONKEY MAN & O'BRIEN CANON. AND IT WAS CUTE!

KEVIN EASTMAN:
FORGET THE ORIGINAL COMICS, THE CARTOON SHOWS, THE THREE MOVIES, BECOMING ENOUGH TOYS AND LICENSED PRODUCTS TO "BREAK" ANY HOUSEHOLD BUDGET, WORLD WIDE FAME, FORTUNE, GROUPIES, AND...WELL YOU GET THE PICTURE...BEING IN GEN13 WAS THE HIGHLIGHT OF OUR CAREER! REALLY-- HONEST, IT WAS! (PSSST-- BY THE WAY, THE LAST ROYALTY CHECK IS LATE...OUR PEOPLE WILL BE IN TOUCH.)
MIKE ALLRED:
IT'S A PARTY 'TWEEN THE PAGES. WEE-HAH!
JEFF SMITH:
IT WAS A BLAST TO BE PART OF A BIG COMIC BOOK EVENT AND IT WAS ALSO FUN TO SEE MY CHARACTERS DRAWN BY SOMEBODY ELSE. THIS CROSSOVER WAS DONE TOTALLY IN THE SPIRIT OF FUN AND ALL OF THE CHARACTERS, NOT JUST BONE, WERE TREATED WITH THE HIGHEST RESPECT.
TERRY MOORE:
KATCHOO IN GEN13 LAND?! THAT'S A SHOCK... BUT A GOOD ONE.
BILLY TUCCI:
I CONSIDERED IT AN HONOR TO BE ASKED TO PARTICIPATE IN GEN13 #13, AND TO HAVE AN ARTIST AS TALENTED AS JEFF CAMPBELL DRAW SHI WAS A THRILL. THIS INDUSTRY COULD USE A LOT MORE BOOKS THAT CAPTURE THE SPIRIT OF FUN DISPLAYED IN THIS COMIC. WHEN CAN WE DO IT AGAIN?

LARRY MARDER:
MY CHARACTERS BRIEF ENCOUNTER WITH THE GEN13 GANG WAS INCREDIBLY FUN. THE BEANS ARE HARDER TO DRAW THEN THEY LOOK AND JEFF AND ALEX DID A GREAT JOB IN CAPTURING THEIR LIKENESSES. I'D DO IT AGAIN IN AN INSTANT.
BOB HARRAS:
I WOULDN'T LEND MY FAVORITE CHARACTER TO JUST ANYONE. BUT WHEN STAN LEE CALLS, YOU CAN'T...HUH? THE OTHER ONE? OH, AHEM, WHEN MY OLD PAL JIM LEE CALLS, YOU KNOW THE ANSWER WILL ALWAYS BE YES!
TODD McFARLANE:
GEN13 WAS THE FIRST COMIC BOOK TO SUCCESSFULLY "AMERICANIZE" THE JAPANESE ANIME COMIC BOOK PHILOSOPHY AND STYLE, SUBSEQUENTLY OPENING UP THE MARKET HERE FOR OTHERS TO FOLLOW. A TRENDSETTER.
SAM KIETH:
ARE YOU SURE MAXX WAS IN THIS BOOK? I HOPE HE DIDN'T CAUSE YOU GUYS ANY TROUBLE, CAUSE WHEN HE SHOWS UP IN MY BOOK HE ALWAYS CONFUSES THE PLOT (LIKE THAT'S POSSIBLE).